About This Book

This book is one that consists of philosophies and business strategies that focus on bringing you freedom, both emotionally and financially; it holds the potential to motivate and inspire you. Everything written in this book comes from my own personal experiences and is worded in a way that makes it simple for anyone to understand. It covers topics like running a business, credit cards, debt, the importance of exercise, working a job, financial struggles, college, and plenty of other important things that can either build or break your overall happiness. Everything is divided into its respective category so you can easily find and read about each topic. Whether you're a young student who is looking for answers or a working adult who wants to learn something new, this small book holds wisdom that can set you free!

Table of Contents

9-5 Jobs

Nothing like getting up every single morning to a job you hate with people you hate to earn a salary you hate. Hate, hate, hate; we all hate our job. Did you know that over 85% of Americans hate their job? That's not very surprising, right?

It's extremely common for me to get on social media and see someone complain about their job. Sometimes I visit stores or restaurants and the employees will carry a bad attitude for no reason! We've all been brainwashed to think that this is the way life is supposed to be. From a young age we're told that we need to stay in school so we can go to college and work for the rest of our lives. Not once do we stop to question ourselves about where our life is going or what we're accomplishing by working that job.

Remember back when you were a child and your parents told you to chase your dreams? What happened to that? Reality, perhaps? Wrong! Your own self-doubt! Think about it: if you hate your job so much then why haven't you quit already? People don't quit their job not because they can't, but because they don't want to. Your own-self-doubt is what's stopping you from quitting; you doubt you'll find a better job if you quit the one you hate. Your brain releases these emotions of fear and self-doubt, resulting in a feeling of hopelessness and feeling stuck with your current job.

As humans, we love mediocrity. We love following the same routine every single day just because it feels safe and secure. Anything out of the ordinary triggers fear and uncertainty in us. By staying in that comfort zone, you are only holding yourself back from better opportunities. You're not growing as a human.

I want you to think about any successful person right now. CEO, actor, musician, athlete — anyone. What do they all have in common? They took risks and constantly stepped out of their comfort zone. You're stuck with the job you hate because you're afraid to take a risk. Guess what? If you don't take that risk, you'll never be able to leave your job. You get out what you put in, that's life. You can't expect your job to magically get any better by complaining about it; action must be taken.

If you hate your job, it's completely your fault. It's not the employer's fault, it's not the salary's fault, it's not the schedule's fault — it's YOUR fault. I know that sounds harsh to say but it's the ultimate truth. Change begins with you. You need to take that leap of faith and quit your job. No one else can do that for you except yourself. Stop making excuses and do something about it.

There was once a story about a young boy who was playing in the woods when he suddenly got bit by a snake. This snake left a painful wound in the boy's leg that made it harder to walk. The wound was left untreated and the effects grew worse and worse until the young boy became a man. Every morning, the man took a short and straight trail to work. Limping and struggling through this trail every morning made the man want to search for an antidote that would heal his leg. One day, the man discovered another trail. This trail looked rough, dangerous, long, and dark. The man finally decided to take this trail one day just to see where it would lead to. He followed this trail for hours until his leg was in excruciating pain. He walked and walked until off in the distance, there was a chest. In this chest, the man found an antidote that healed his leg and brought him many years of happiness and vitality.

As you can tell from this story, the man was brave enough to take a risk and travel into the unknown. If the man didn't take the unknown trail, he would've lived the rest of his life limping in pain. By working an awful job, you are basically damaging yourself, both mentally and physically. Think about it: you get home exhausted, hungry, and maybe even angry. The only way to let go of these burdens is by changing your mindset.

When all is said and done, life is what you make of it. If you work at a fast-food restaurant but want to be a famous musician, then practice. Take classes, learn from other musicians, perform in small venues, travel in search of opportunities. Maybe you work in an office but want to be your own boss; read a lot of books, learn the rules, get a valuable and marketable skill, go to networking events. Any goal is possible when you work hard and truly want it.

The amazing thing about this era is that our lives revolve around technology and social media. This means that millions of opportunities are available for us simply by looking online. This world is driven by knowledge and creativity. If you possess both skills, you can do what you love all while making a living. Almost all of us have creativity, but not all of us have the knowledge we need in order to leave. Ignorance and fear are ultimately what keep us chained to our dreaded jobs.

Did you know that the average lifespan of a human is 79 years? That's right, humans have lifespans. So why is it that millions of us waste our lives doing something we hate? You're not immortal; you're slowly dying every single day. As morbid as that sounds, it's a fact. Instead of making the most out of life, why are you wasting your time and energy on what you hate the most? Why are you just letting life pass you by?

Don't misconstrue my message; I'm not telling you to head into work tomorrow morning and throw your name tag on the ground and then walk out. That would be a stupid idea. What I'm telling you to do is turn your passion into a job that pays. This means that you'll be working twice as hard. You'll be working the job you hate but you'll also be working on what you love. You want to get to the point where your passion is bringing in a sustainable and consistent income so you can finally grow the confidence to leave your job and focus on what you truly want.

In other words, you need to bust your ass off on what you want in order to make it your main source of income. Start investing ALL your passion and energy into what you love the most. When you're living off what you love, it doesn't even feel like a "job." Why? Because it's something you enjoy doing, so it doesn't feel tedious or pointless.

At the end of the day, you're in charge of your life and you get to decide what happens. If you're comfortable with mediocrity and constantly making excuses for everything, then do that for the rest of your life. If you want to be successful and do what you love, then work hard for it every single day. Plan, write down your goals, and get ready to work twice as hard in order to achieve those dreams.

If it was easy, then everybody would be doing what they love. It's hard, so we settle for mediocrity and take the road without risk. Life doesn't just hand out opportunities for free; you need to be willing to make sacrifices in order to reach your goals. You need be willing to fall a million times and get back up every single time. This is the only life you got. You're breathing right now, and the clock is ticking. Chase what you want or don't. The choice is yours to make, so go ahead and decide.

Credit Cards and Debt

A card that lets us spend whatever we want until the end of the month? That sounds great! What could possibly go wrong? Quite a lot. Did you know that the total credit card debt in the United States is over $1 trillion? That says a lot about American consumers. A lot of our suffering and stress comes from debt. We owe money but money is what we need.

We buy things that we can't pay back on time. All for what? Instant gratification. Do you know what would prevent all debt? Patience. After all, that's all debt really is — the inability to be patient enough to afford something, and then buying it with money that you don't have. We do this because it's in our human nature to have things that we desire, instantly and quickly.

Everyone wants money, but no one wants to work for it. Credit cards are the easy way out. They give us the ability to buy things with someone else's money and then pay for them at the end of the month. That feels good to us because it's not our money, so who cares? I want you to imagine yourself in the following scenario:

You're at the store and you see a brand-new TV for $800. You really want it, so you go ahead and purchase it with your credit card. Now you own a new TV!

That seems easy and painless, right? Now imagine buying that exact same TV for the same price but having to pay with cash. Now it feels painful and you feel your wallet aching; you might even feel buyer's remorse. Why is that? Well, maybe the idea of having to stand there and physically count out $800 might have something to do with it.

This has to do with our brain reacting to what we're holding. If you're paying with a credit card, it's just a piece of plastic. You swipe it and then put it back in your pocket, simple. When you pay with cash, that's YOUR money. You know how hard you worked for that money, so it's difficult for you to let go of it. Debit cards are in the middle; they're just plastic that you swipe but it's your own money. In conclusion, paying with cash triggers the most pain, then debit cards, and finally credit cards. Out of sight, out of mind. Try this out the next time you make a purchase.

Do I think you should get a credit card? Absolutely not! Getting a credit card is a recipe for disaster, especially if you're someone who is irresponsible; all the "perks" that come with a credit card lead you to believe that getting one is an obvious choice, but it's not that simple! Cash back rewards? Travel rewards? That sounds great, doesn't it? Wrong!

All of those "rewards" are minuscule compared to the amount of money you must spend for them to become significant. People who constantly use credit cards swear by their "rewards." You're not saving anything. How can you be saving money if the money you're using isn't yours in the first place? Do you seriously think you can outsmart a multi-billion-dollar company who studies human behavior? Companies pressure you into getting a credit card by implementing their "rewards" and stressing the importance of needing good credit in order to buy a house or a car.

Buying something you can't afford is NEVER a smart decision. ALWAYS buy in cash; cash gives you complete purchasing power. When was the last time someone got rich and successful by using a credit card's "travel rewards?" Cash is and will always be king. You need cash in order to make more cash.

You don't get a credit card to save money because if that was the case, then everyone with a credit card would be a millionaire. You get a credit card because you want the power to buy things instantly, even if you can't afford them. You get a credit card because you want to avoid the pain you feel when paying with cash. You get a credit card to build up your credit score in order to get a house or car you can't afford. Why are you getting something unaffordable? Here's the secret to avoiding debt:

Be patient, earn up enough money, and then make the purchase.

That's it! It's not a huge, sophisticated formula. The reason people are in debt isn't because they didn't follow that advice – they're in debt because they felt the need to make a big and stupid purchase in order to impress family, friends, and random strangers.

We're living in a world where everyone wants the latest technology and the newest cars. We want these things because they give us a false sense of pride. We want these things because we want to impress the neighbor next door. We want these things because we feel that others will look down on us if we don't have them. Here's a little reality check:

No one cares.

No one cares what you're driving or wearing because everyone else is busy doing their own thing. The world doesn't revolve around you. Why is it that we're quick to laugh at others who don't have the newest car or the biggest home? Meanwhile, we're drowning in a pool of debt with cars and houses that the bank owns. We're afraid to live frugally because we fear judgment. We don't want others to see that we're struggling or living poorly. We feel ashamed and embarrassed.

There's an old quote by Henry Ward Beecher that goes:

"He is rich or poor according to what he is, not according to what he has."

Humility builds wealth, not the other way around. If you want to become rich and successful, you can't live rich now and expect to stay rich later; you're supposed to live humbly now so you can live better later. A lot of us do the opposite – we live "rich" now but later in life we fall into a pool of debt that humbles us and makes us pay for our foolish actions.

Debt exists and we're aware that it exists. We know people that are in debt and hear about it all the time. Why is it that we follow those exact same habits and footsteps? Look at it this way: you see millions of people playing with fire and they end up burning themselves. You then decide it's a good idea to join them and experience it first-hand, despite knowing exactly what will happen.

That sounds incredibly stupid, right? That's what we do all the time when we decide to get a credit card. We know the repercussions of it, yet we still decide it's a good idea.

If you're in debt right now, stop using your credit card immediately. Tear it apart and get rid of it. How do you expect to get out of debt by using what got you there in the first place? The debt isn't going to just magically disappear, so you need to sit down and write a budget. You're going to be living poorly until you pay off your debt. This means that you won't be eating out at restaurants, you won't be going to the movies, you won't be shopping. You can't buy anything except for food and necessities — that's it. You must be willing to sacrifice your lavish lifestyle in order to get rid of this financial burden. Stick to your budget until your debt is finally paid off and never get a credit card again. Irresponsible actions lead to inevitable consequences.

If you don't own a credit card, good; don't get one. Wealth is built with cash and cash only. If you use a credit card, then you don't want to be rich. Who would you rather take advice from, a millionaire who built his wealth on cash or your next-door neighbor working a 9-5 job telling you how much money their credit card has saved them? I'd much rather listen to the millionaire.

I'm not telling you to live your entire life frugally. What fun would that be? Life is about enjoying everything; if you're afraid to let go of your money, then why are you working for it in the first place? Buy the necessities you need to survive but go ahead and buy luxuries that you can afford every now and then. At the end of the day, YOU control your money. YOU get to decide how that money is used and where it all goes. That's also why it's crucial for you to know how to manage, invest, and spend.

Debit cards are also a great alternative to cash because it's still your money, only in a plastic form. Debit cards have the exact same protection as credit cards. The zero-liability policy covers all credit card AND debit card transactions processed over the Visa network. Using a debit card also comes with responsibilities. You need to keep your PIN safe, constantly check your bank statement, and make sure you don't lose it.

Ultimately, you want to have a plan for saving and spending. You need a budget. Without a budget, you're just handling money blindly. Split your budget into needs, wants, and savings. The best feeling ever is financial freedom. Not owing anyone money removes a lot of weight off your shoulders and contributes to your overall happiness and lifestyle. Debt is NEVER a good thing, so avoid it at all costs. A credit card will never make you rich, remember that.

The Costs of College

For many of us, college is where we go after graduating from high school; we depend on a degree in order to get a high-paying career. In the United States, over 44 million Americans hold nearly $1.5 trillion in student debt; that means around one in four Americans are paying off student loans.

Do you go to college? If so, why? If not, do you plan on going? If you already graduated from college, how was it? Many of us think that we need college in order to be successful — after all, that's what we prepare for all throughout high school, right? Not necessarily. You see, the school system follows a certain curriculum that prepares you for college. You learn subjects like mathematics, English, biology, American history, and things of that nature.

School doesn't teach you how to change a tire or close a sale. Because you only learn college-applicable skills in high school, you have no other option but to attend college when you graduate. Why? Because grammar and equations are all you know. It's not your fault or the school's.

There are three types of intelligence: analytical intelligence, creative intelligence, and practical intelligence. Analytical intelligence is what we learn in school; it focuses on academic problem-solving. Creative intelligence deals with using your imagination in order to solve a problem or make something. Good examples of this would be creating an invention, making a beautiful painting, or creating poetry that is capable of triggering the emotions. Lastly, we have practical intelligence. This intelligence is more often referred to as "street smarts" and common sense. This is the intelligence needed in order to survive and be successful.

Unfortunately, this is also the intelligence that not too many of us have. It seems that common sense isn't so common nowadays. Practical intelligence focuses on things like communication skills, everyday problems, and knowing how society functions. If you want to convince an employer, you're not going to sit there and read a poem or show them that you know the quadratic formula. Employers don't care that you have a degree; they just want to know if you have experience and know how to solve everyday problems. What do you have to offer that others don't?

Practical intelligence isn't something that you can learn through books or a class. You learn practical intelligence by stepping outside your house and interacting with others. As you start interacting with more and more people, you begin to pick up patterns and start to understand how certain individuals behave and why they behave that way.

The problem with this is that no one socializes anymore! Everyone communicates through their phones, so it's difficult to interact with other humans. The amazing thing about practical intelligence is that you can learn it anywhere simply by observing the world and interacting with others.

So, what does all of this have to do with college? Should you just drop out of high school? No. The point I'm getting across is that college isn't for everyone. If you want to work in the medical field, go to college. If you want to pursue law, go to college. College is usually required for these types of careers. There are thousands of good-paying jobs you can get without a degree. We don't go to college because we want to, we go because we feel pressured to — either by friends, parents, or our own doubts. Then what usually ends up happening? We start complaining about our professors, our college work, and our student loans.

The thing about a public high school is that it's free. You're allowed to complain and miss class at no cost. You go because it's mandatory. College is different because it costs money; you're attending classes that YOU chose to pay for. If you're passionate about your major, then great! On the other hand, if you're constantly complaining about college and always missing class, then you need to sit down and have a serious talk with yourself. Why are you burning money for something you're not passionate about? What made you choose to attend college in the first place? Conformity? Friends?

You need to figure out if going to college will help or hurt you. It's normal to not know what you want to do once you graduate high school. Don't let fear cause you to make an impulsive decision that'll make you fall into debt. Explore yourself. Figure out what you love to do and find out how you can turn that into a career.

When I was in high school, I was a naturally gifted student. I had a high analytical intelligence even though I rarely ever applied myself or studied. It was just easy for me to grasp things quickly and get good grades. Amazing, right? Not really. Throughout my high school years, I was afraid because I KNEW that my analytical intelligence didn't mean anything in the real world. Because of this, I had no idea what I wanted to do after high school. Everyone was applying for universities while I was doing nothing. Then, during my last months in high school, I had an epiphany.

I can do anything once I graduate. This is MY life.

After I graduated, I did exactly that. I wrote a book and then attended a community college to get my Associate degree in Computer Programming and Technology. Did I go so I could get a job afterwards?

Nope! I went in order to learn a valuable skill that could be applied to my life. After learning this skill, I started my own web design business. Even if anything happens to my business, I can still turn to my degree and get a temporary job if I need to. If you went back in time to when I was in high school and told me that I would one day be running my own business, I would've thought you were crazy.

I share this personal story so you can see that it's okay to be afraid and uncertain about your future. Everyone in this world is lost and searching for answers. The important thing is working to find the answers in order to figure out what you want. Question yourself. If you're a high school student, take a moment to figure out if college is really for you. If you're a college student, take a moment to figure out if you're going because you're passionate, or if you're just going for the sake of it.

If you graduated from college and owe thousands in student loans, take a moment to figure out if college was worth it. You owe money, but are you happy with your degree and career? Are you able to pay off the student loans with ease?

Deciding whether to attend college or not is a huge decision that shouldn't be taken lightly or done impulsively. Here are some signs that maybe college isn't for you:

1: You feel like it's a waste of money.

2: Your desire to explore is strong.

3: You know you can make it without a degree.

4: Going to college feels like you're just doing it for your parents.

5: You feel lost in life.

6: To you, work experience is more important than education.

7: You just don't feel like it.

If you're wondering how to attend college without falling into debt, the answer is simple: go to a community college. It might seem like obvious advice, but you'd be surprised how many people don't do this; instead, they graduate from high school and go straight to a university. Unless you have a scholarship, you're just wasting money. What you want to do is graduate from high school, attend a two-year community college, and THEN transfer to a four-year university.

Don't go to a certain college or university just to join your friends or make your family proud. A college doesn't define you. I've met community college graduates who went on to do big things; I've also met university graduates who are drowning in student loans and can't seem to find a job. No college is less or more than another. There's nothing prestigious or smart about owing thousands in student loans.

Ultimately, college isn't for everyone. It's a waste of time for some people and super beneficial for others. Some use what they learned to land a career and others use what they learned to start their own business. Knowledge is knowledge. You should strive to learn something new every day. As Ben Franklin once said:

"An investment in knowledge pays the best interest."

Make it a commitment to sharpen your intelligence every day. Use your imagination to express your creative intelligence. Read some books to expand your analytical intelligence. Communicate with others to master practical intelligence. Life is all about learning; the more you know, the better. Whether you pay for knowledge or find it online for free, it doesn't matter. Just learn. Your mind is like a sponge that loves to absorb all sorts of new information.

Starting a Business

You've learned how to quit your job, the dangers of a credit card, and how important street smarts are. Now I'm going to show you how to start a business. This chapter covers the basics and fundamentals of starting a business, while the next chapter talks about business strategies and techniques.

Whenever someone tells you that they run a business, what usually comes to mind? Wealth? Suits? Success? Freedom? The truth is, businesses are all around us. While owning a business gives you freedom, it isn't necessarily an indicator of success. There are good businesses and bad businesses. Contrary to popular belief, having your own business isn't an accomplishment; anyone can start a business, including a small child without any knowledge.

Any kid can go outside and put up a lemonade stand. You know what IS an accomplishment? Having a SUCCESSFUL business.

So, what exactly is a business? A business is any organization where goods or services are exchanged for money. Every business relies on demand and value. If people don't want it, they won't buy it. If people don't see the value in it, they won't buy it. If no one buys, your business will fail. A business is a business, but not all businesses are the same. Running a sales team requires a different skill set than running a coffee shop. If you run a coffee shop, you're not going to be cold calling people to try your coffee.

Because of this, every business should be treated uniquely. The eight steps I'm about to give you will show you the basics and fundamentals on how to start a business. Learn and take in whatever works for YOU.

STEP 1: DO YOUR RESEARCH.

Starting a business is exciting; your brain is racing with so many ideas and visions. You're ready to get started but you don't quite know where or how to start. Well, the first thing you need to do is research. You need to learn all about the type of business you'll be running. This is crucial in order to create a successful and lasting business.

Before you even decide to start a business, you should already have experience in that field. If you're starting a web design business, you should already have experience with making websites. If you're going to open a coffee shop, you should already know how to make an amazing cup of coffee. If you're going to start a photography business, you should already know the important fundamentals. Research your business online and find out if there's demand and potential for it to grow.

STEP 2: PLAN IT OUT.

Once you've done enough research and you're certain that this business has the potential to thrive, you need to create a game plan. How do you think architects design buildings? Through the mind? No! They make detailed blueprints that show the process of everything. You need to have a plan in order to turn your business idea into a reality.

Sit down and write down everything you need for your new business. Will you need help from others? Do you need a POS system to process transactions? Is your business going to have a physical location or will your services be offered online? You want to make a list of all your needs in order to build your business properly. You can't build a home if a few bricks are missing — the house will collapse. This step is probably one of the most crucial when creating a business.

STEP 3: DO YOUR FINANCES.

Starting your own business sounds exciting until you're faced with reality and realize that since this is your own business, YOU are responsible for handling everything. YOU are responsible for paying taxes. YOU are responsible for setting your prices. YOU are responsible for setting your own salary. Depending on your type of business, YOU might also be responsible for getting a capital.

Since you are the owner and don't get a paycheck, no one withholds income tax or self-employment tax from what you take out. Because of this, you are required to pay these taxes quarterly. That's right, four times a year. Don't feel intimidated! All business owners do this. If you're confused about this, research it or feel free to speak to a tax professional. This saves you a lot of time, money, and headaches.

STEP 4: CREATE A STRUCTURE.

For a business to operate smoothly, you need to create a structure. How will you deliver your service? How will you promote your business? Who will oversee certain things? What you're doing here is figuring out where all the building blocks go and how they will operate. This will be different for every business.

I own a web design business, so my structure is simple and straightforward. I create web pages for businesses. This is done by making appointments with business owners and getting together with them. I have contracts in place and I also have a portfolio to showcase my work. I charge an initial payment and a final payment. I know my target audience. This is structure; everything is detailed, organized, and done in a certain way. Design a structure for your business.

STEP 5: PICK A BUSINESS NAME.

This is a step that you want to spend a lot of time on. The name of your business reflects what you do and who you are. Choosing a poor business name can make the difference between failure and success. A common mistake people make when creating a business name is being too plain. If your name doesn't stand out, people won't find you. Be creative.

Don't name your business after yourself. Another mistake to avoid is creating a long business name. You want your business name to be meaningful, unique, powerful, and clever. Grab a piece of paper and write down all the names you have in mind. Start by crossing out the ones that aren't good. Once you're left with two or three names, think about those. Don't decide immediately. Think on it for a few days until you're confident on the one you'll choose.

STEP 6: GET A WEBSITE.

As a web designer, I can't stress this step enough. Having a website for your business is crucial for it to expand and reach a bigger audience. Did you know that 30% of consumers won't consider a business without a website? We're living in a world where everyone is connected to the Internet, so you'd think that it'd be common sense to get a website.

A website gives your business social proof and it makes you stand out. It makes it convenient for customers to easily find everything online and it's an amazing way to stay in touch with them. The worst mistake business owners make is trying to create their own website. Let me ask you this: would you buy a car designed by an engineer or an everyday person? Don't cheap out on this step! Hire a professional web designer who wants to help your business grow and expand!

STEP 7: PROMOTE YOUR BUSINESS.

Now that you've launched your business, you want to attract clients. The days of attaching flyers to walls are over — the Internet is your best tool for promoting your business. In order to get more people to notice your business, you want to be on social media platforms. Tell your friends and family about your business.

If you're a freelancer, find ways to make your portfolio get bigger. A portfolio showcases your work and it shows potential clients that you have the experience needed in order to deliver your service.

Find ways to attract more clients and grow your business name. Talk to people who run successful businesses and ask them how they promote themselves. Look online and see how other businesses promote themselves; learn and see what works and what doesn't work.

STEP 8: DON'T GIVE UP.

Running a business gives you the freedom to set your own schedule and salary. You get to make the decisions. On the downside, running a business isn't easy. It requires responsibility and consistency. If you're a freelancer, it's SUPER easy to slack off because you have no one telling you what to do. Businesses take a long time to grow — they don't happen overnight.

When I first started my web design business, I didn't find any clients for the first few months. I worked hard and learned from my mistakes until I was able to get my first client. All you need is ONE sale to give you the confidence boost you need for your business to take off. The key is to learn from your mistakes and not give up. Customers are out there; you just need to find the perfect way to attract them. Never give up and always do your best.

Sales Strategies

So now that you know how to start a business, it's important for you to understand how businesses influence and attract customers. In order to achieve this, we need to understand human behavior and how it works. There are two parts to a business: running the business and then being able to sell your service. What do I mean by that? You can be the best graphic designer on Earth but if you don't know how to sell your service, your business will fail. I create websites but if I don't know how to add value to them, what good are my skills?

This whole chapter focuses on sales strategies that you can apply to your business in order to close more sales. The important thing here is to actually learn and apply these tips and strategies to your business.

COLD CALLING.

How many times have you been doing something when suddenly your phone rings? You don't know who it is, but you answer anyways. Next thing you know, someone is trying to force a product or service down your throat. You lost your train of thought and now you're irritated. Don't you just hate when that happens?

This is essentially what cold calling is; you're calling strangers in order to sell your product or service. This is probably one of the worst techniques used in business. Despite this, millions of businesses and companies still rely on cold calling in order to close sales. The problem with this method is that you don't know what the other person is doing when you call them. They might be having dinner with their family or they might be in a hospital. It's annoying and forced. Whenever I get a call from a salesman, I want to hang up.

It's obvious to see that you don't care who I am or what my needs are — you're just trying to sell me a product or service. Imagine that you're walking through the mall and someone comes up to you and starts offering you a product — that person is interrupting your routine.

I'm not saying that you should never cold call; you just need to change the way you see and approach cold calling. In order to do this, you need to understand the other person's needs. Before you call them, you need to know who they are and what they do. You need to figure out their problems in order to offer a valuable solution. You want to research the person or company you're calling and try to learn as much as you can about them. Showing someone that you took the time to learn about them or their company goes a long way. It tells them that you care and that you have a solution to their problems. Do your research first.

Once you know exactly who you're going to be calling, you want to make it clear that you know them right from the second they answer. Don't greet them with meaningless questions like:

"Hey, how are you? Is this [name here]?"

This is the approach many people take. The first question is empty, and the second question is ridiculous. It makes it seem like you're unsure who you're talking to. There's one thing everyone in this world values the most. Do you know what that thing is?

Time.

People value time. They hate when you waste their time. If you're not offering something of value, you're wasting their time. If you're not offering a solution, you're wasting their time. Lack of time is the main reason why cold calling usually fails.

Think about it: you don't know what the other person is doing. Because of this, you don't have their full attention. This person has never heard of you before and they don't know what you look like; do you know what that means? There's a lack of trust. You can't close a sale with someone who isn't giving you their full attention. You can't close a sale with someone who doesn't trust you. If some random stranger offered you a drink, would you take it? Probably not. You don't trust them because you've never met them before.

Even if you have amazing communication skills, cold calling is still difficult. You can't close a sale in a short amount of time. You can't gain someone's trust in a short amount of time. Don't cold call with the intention of closing a sale — you can't. Cold call in order to try and set up an appointment with the business owner. Even then, this technique should only be used as a last resort.

What should you do then? Well, there's an alternative and more modern method: cold emailing. It's essentially the same as cold calling, except you're not interrupting the person. They get the freedom of replying to you whenever they have the chance. Cold emailing is a method that takes a lot of practice because you're essentially trying to captivate someone's interest by only using words.

Although cold emailing is a better alternative, there are also mistakes you want to avoid. The most common mistake is sending the exact same email to everyone, just with a different greeting. This looks like spam and the recipient will immediately notice. Again, take the time to research and learn about the person you're contacting.

The second mistake a lot of people make is sending an email that's way too long to read.

Don't get me wrong, showing the recipient that you understand their needs is great, but don't send them a long email. It's a waste of time for both of you. On top of that, it sounds like you're trying too hard to influence them. The longer your email is, the lower your chances are for a reply. I learned this the hard way when I first started cold emailing businesses. I used to send long emails detailing everything I offered and most of the time, I wouldn't hear back from them. Eventually I decided to change my approach and send an email with one or two meaningful questions, and I immediately noticed that more people began to reply.

The key with cold emailing is to experiment. You want to see what triggers a response and what doesn't. Don't overthink it — all you want is for the person to reply. Remember, the goal isn't to close the sale; you're trying to set up an appointment with the owner. Practice makes perfect.

The more you fail, the easier it becomes to see why. Mastery is only attained through failure.

Cold calling and cold emailing are two of the main ways to grow if you're starting off as a freelancer. In the beginning, no one is going to come to you for your service. You need to get out there and make a name for yourself. People won't come to you until you have an audience; they need to hear others talk about your work before they consider coming to you.

The best way to practice cold emailing is to do it. Start off with small businesses and work your way up to bigger ones. Not everyone is going to say "yes." Most people will usually say "no" in the beginning. Don't lose hope! Once you get used to hearing that word a lot, you'll feel a lot more comfortable selling your service because you no longer feel the fear of rejection.

CONTRAST PRICING PSYCHOLOGY.

Let's say that you go to the movie theaters and you want to buy some popcorn. There are three sizes to choose from: small, regular, and large. You end up buying regular-sized popcorn. This powerful technique is called "contrast pricing." Still confused? Let's dive deeper and look at it under a microscope.

When you're offering a service to somebody, the whole goal is to get them to buy from you. You want to influence the person by offering value to your service or product. An amazing way to do this is through contrast pricing. Let's say that you're a fitness trainer and offer a monthly training program to your clients; let's call this "Program A." Program A costs $700 a month. It includes 8 workout sessions and a simple meal plan. This is the only training program you offer, so now answer this question: what options are there?

That's right, none! You only offer Plan A, so the potential client is probably thinking something like:

"Do I want to buy this product, or do I not want buy this product?"

You don't want that! You want to give your customers choices! Now let's say that you've had Plan A for a while but now you also decide to add a Plan B. Plan B costs $1,000 a month and it includes 15 workout sessions, a dedicated meal plan, free membership to 1 gym, a free digital weight scale, 2 pounds of protein powder, access to a nutrition-tracking app, and a free shirt.

Now you have two training programs to choose from, so now the potential client is thinking differently; they're no longer thinking whether they want it or not because now their brain saying something like:

"I get two options! Do I want to buy Plan A, or do I want to buy Plan B?"

See, now you're giving the client a choice to choose between one thing or another. That's good, but we want to add in one more training program; let's add Plan C to the mix. Plan C costs $3,000 and it includes 30 workout sessions, a dedicated meal plan, free access to EVERY gym in your town, a free digital weight scale, a food scale with measuring cups, 4 pounds of protein powder, access to a nutrition-tracking app, a free shirt, 24/7 access to a live nutrition expert, and a watch to monitor your footsteps and heartbeat.

How crazy does that sound? Now that you have three choices, your client gets to decide which plan they want, except you already know which plan it is. About 60% of your clients will opt for Plan B. Why? Read over all the plans again. Plan A includes 2 things; it's small and doesn't have much to offer. Plan C includes 10 things; it has an outrageous price but comes with so many amazing things.

Finally, look at Plan B. Plan B includes 7 things. It offers the best value. It's not too small and it's not too expensive. Plan A looks too "weak" and Plan C is outrageous. Occasionally, you'll get a client who wants the biggest and the best, so they'll opt for Plan C. You're not trying to sell Plan C though; it's a decoy. Two choices are good, but three choices are the best. Anything more than that and it becomes confusing for everyone.

This is essentially how contrast pricing works. You trick the mind from deciding whether it wants it or not, to deciding which one it wants. By implementing this powerful technique into your business, you drastically increase the chances of selling something as opposed to nothing at all. Remember, humans love choices. We don't like being forced to choose from one thing. Selling is all about adding as much value as you can to your product.

IDENTIFYING TARGET CUSTOMERS.

In the world of business, you'll come across hundreds of people all the time. If you work in sales, then it's important for you to understand the people you're working with.

The more people you meet, you more you start to pick up on certain personality patterns. Someone might buy your product instantly while others desperately try to find a bargain. You might think that selling to as many people as possible is the point of business, and while that's partially true, there ARE some people who you want to avoid doing business with. These are either people who don't respect the value of your work or want to waste your time.

In this part, we're going to be going over the four main types of customers, how to sell to them, and which ones you should avoid. This will save you valuable time and help you focus on the serious buyers.

The first type of customer you'll encounter is the cheapskate. This is the person who doesn't care about the value of your work; the only thing this person cares about is the price. The more money they save, the better. These types of customers want the cheapest option their money can buy. If that's not available, then they'll try their hardest to get a bargain. Sometimes, they'll ask how much you charge before you even get the chance to show them your value.

The problem is, even if you try to show them your value, they STILL won't buy from you. Why? It's in their DNA to be cheap. In their eyes, if they're not saving money, they're losing. Don't confuse cheap customers with customers who can't afford your service. It's possible to sell to customers who can't afford your service; it's impossible to sell to customers who only see price. Make sure your business doesn't attract these types of customers.

The next type of customer in the world of sales is the confident customer. These customers know exactly what they want and how they want it. They have the money to buy and the knowledge to decide. Confident customers will ask you a lot of solid questions pertaining to your product or service in order to learn more. A lot of times, you can't close a sale immediately with these customers; they'll tell you they need time to think or decide. Don't confuse this with the type of customers who just say that as a polite way of saying "no thanks."

If you're new to sales or interacting with others, this customer might seem like the most intimidating at first because they'll surprise you with good questions. Don't confuse interest with doubt! They're asking because they're interested in your service or product. Confident customers are usually the ones who you gain the most experience from.

Next, we have the most annoying people you can encounter: the demanding customer. These are the customers no one wants to deal with. They'll doubt your value, challenge you, waste your time, and demand unrealistic goals. Worst of all, they never buy your service or product! To them, everything revolves around skepticism. They'll ask meaningless questions and find ways to refute you. You can present all the logical facts about your service or product and they'll STILL question your value.

Customers like this don't know what they want. They're the most difficult to deal with because they make no sense. Demanding customers are like people who go to a fast-food restaurant and can't decide what to get; they hold up everyone else who is hungry and knows what they want. These customers are the biggest time-killers and should be avoided at all costs.

Lastly, we have the emotional customer. This customer doesn't mind the price of your service or product. These customers don't care about logical facts because they buy based solely with their feelings. Emotional customers observe how you behave and treat them; they want to buy from someone who they trust and like. If they smell something fishy, they'll take a step back. Don't try to educate these customers about your product or service — THEY DON'T CARE. They just want to know if they can trust you!

Emotional customers require you to have charisma and strong communication skills. Don't try to sell to them; talk to them like a friend and trigger their emotions. Gain their trust and show them that you're a loyal person. These are often the easiest and best customers to sell to because they usually just require confidence and charisma. If their heart truly wants it, they'll buy it.

COMMUNICATION SKILLS.

In the world of business, communication and the power to influence is EVERYTHING. If you're not good at communicating with others, then your business will fail. The whole industry of business requires strong practical intelligence. Remember that term from earlier? You need a strong understanding for human behavior if you want to persuade people to buy your service or product.

Selling is just the art of persuading someone to buy from you — that's it. Think about it: why do you buy anything? You've been persuaded into thinking that you needed it. Persuasion is the most important skill you need when running a business. Learning how to persuade someone isn't just something that you can learn in one day; this powerful communication skill takes years of practice and experience.

Psychology plays a huge role in business because you need to understand your customer's needs. Although every human is different and unique, there are quite a few things that everyone has in common.

One of the first things everyone has in common is the tendency to lie. That's right, customers will lie to you! Why would they lie to you? Well, there are several possibilities; the first is out of respect. What do I mean by that? Let's say that someone offers you a dish that you've never tried before and it doesn't look too appetizing. Instead of telling them that it looks disgusting, you tell them that you're not hungry. You're not lying to them with hurtful intentions, but simply out of respect. Customers do this all the time.

The worst thing you can do when you know that a customer is lying is just playing along with them; you'll never close a sale by doing this.

One of the most common lies that you'll hear from customers sounds something like this:

"That sounds great! Just give me some time to think about it and then I'll get back to you in a few days! Thanks for your time though!"

Then what happens? You wait forever and they never get back to you! Customers do this as a polite way of telling you that they're not interested. In order to gain their interest, you need to figure out what the problem is. Instead of falling for this lie and never hearing from them again, be straightforward and direct. Say something like this:

"Mr. Client. Can I tell you something? I've worked with a lot of people in the past and a lot of times they tell me that they'll get back to me, but they never do, either because they have doubts or because of the price. Tell me honestly, is that the case right now?"

By addressing the elephant in the room, you're giving the customer a chance to openly tell you what they don't like about your product or service. Once you figure out the problem, you can focus on that and talk to the customer about it.

Look, if you can't close a sale during the first meeting, you're not going to close at all. You get one chance and that's it. Unless the customer genuinely needs time to think about it, they're not going to bother wasting their time contacting you again. Remember, time is what humans value the most. Your goal is to close the sale right then and there.

The problem with most people who are new to the world of business is that they're afraid to take the wheel. Why are you afraid? YOU are the one selling. YOU are the one who's offering value. YOU are the one who should take control of the conversation. Show your confidence.

What separates a good salesman from a bad one? The ability to handle and deal with objections. Selling is all about having an answer for every objection and then knowing how to turn the tables.

Before you even step into that meeting, you need to know every single objection that your customer might use, and you need to have a perfect answer for each one. How can you do this? PRACTICE. PRACTICE, PRACTICE, PRACTICE. Look in the mirror and pretend that you're trying to sell your service. Think of every single objection possible for that service and know how you'll reply. Sit down with a friend or family member and have them play the customer. Practice thousands of times until you know your service or product like the back of your hand. Lying is a defense mechanism. Find out what your customer is doubtful about, address it, and then persuade them with confidence and charisma.

BODY LANGUAGE TECHNIQUES.

Did you know that nonverbal communication is just as important as verbal communication? The difference between good and bad body language can determine whether you close a sale or not. Would you rather trust someone who is talking to you with their eyes on the floor, or someone who is talking to you with their eyes on yours? Chances are, you'll probably choose the latter.

Body language is often a reflection of our own confidence. If you're nervous, you'll tend to look around a lot and constantly tap your foot. If you're frustrated, you might let out a deep breath. All these things play a role in how customers perceive us. You want to have confident body language. A handshake is probably one of the most important pieces of nonverbal communication in business. You can tell just from a handshake whether someone is confident or not.

Look in the mirror and study your body language. Do you move your hands too much when expressing your thoughts? Should you move them more often? Do your facial expressions match your emotions? Does your posture look too stiff? Are your eyes wandering around a lot? Take note of these little details and work on improving them. You want to have confident, open, and friendly body language. If you're not open, it looks like you're hiding something; your customer will notice this, and they won't trust you.

Having strong verbal communication is crucial too. Make sure you speak clearly and confidently. Don't talk like you're a robot. Animate your voice and talk with enthusiasm. Enthusiasm is contagious and it'll get your customer excited as well. Know when to talk fast and when to talk slow. Master the art of verbal and nonverbal communication. Confidence is key.

BUSINESS CARDS.

How many times has someone gave you a business card? What do you usually do with that business card? You throw it away or forget about it, right? A business card is a huge part of your image and it reflects how others perceive you. While some people might think that a glossy and flashy business card makes you look important, others might see you as arrogant. If you hand over a plain and matte business card, some people might think that you're cheap while others might see you as a serious professional.

Now, what if I told you that business cards aren't effective? If you're handing out business cards at a networking event, guess what? So is everyone else. It doesn't matter what type of material or finish you use; business cards don't leave a lasting mark. People usually throw them away and forget about you.

Don't get me wrong, I use business cards sometimes, but there's also another item that I hand out to all my clients. This item is super powerful and effective; it leaves a lasting mark and it's better than a business card. Do you know what that item is? A book. That's right, I hand out books as business cards. Not just any book though — my book. People throw away business cards, but they don't throw away a book. A book carries knowledge and weight. It's powerful. British historian James Bryce once said:

"The worth of a book is to be measured by what you can carry away from it."

People expect business cards, they don't expect a book — especially not a book that YOU published. A book is better than a business card because it offers knowledge. It shows that you know what you're talking about and it makes you stand out from the crowd.

Publishing a book isn't something that you can do overnight, but it's something ANYONE can do. If you're a freelancer, then writing a book is definitely something you should consider. You're not trying to become a best-seller; the goal is to write a book that shows that you're knowledgeable in what you do. Who would you rather do business with, someone who hands you a business card or someone who hands you their book? The answer is pretty obvious.

Although each copy might cost you a few dollars, the lasting impact you'll leave on your customers makes it worth it. I didn't write this book with the intention of selling a million copies; I wrote this book as a way to share my knowledge.

Books date all the way back to the 1450s; they're powerful pieces of history because that knowledge stays in a page even after we die. Having knowledge gives you power.

PRICING.

Let me ask you a question. Would you rather buy a website that costs $200 or $2,000? If you chose the first option, you're probably someone who wants to save money; if you chose the latter option, you're probably someone who prioritizes and respects quality.

When you're pricing your product or service too low, you're attracting cheapskates. Anyone who appreciates quality won't consider you because they'll ask themselves questions like:

"Why is the price so low? What's wrong with it? Is it a low-quality product? What am I paying for?"

It's in our nature to associate low prices with low quality, and high prices with high quality. Don't get me wrong, you can buy amazing things for a low price and you can waste large amounts of money on trash.

The most common problem with people who are new to sales is their pricing. They're afraid to raise the prices of their product or service, so they settle for a low price. You do this because you don't believe in the quality of your work. You're afraid that the customer will think your price is outrageous.

Customers don't pay for a product or service. Do you know what they pay for? Your knowledge and the value that you bring to them. You're putting a price on your knowledge and experience, not your service or product. An amazing example of this is found in the auto mechanics industry. If you need your oil changed but don't know how, you go to a mechanic. Do you know how long an oil change takes? About 15 minutes. You remove the drain plug, catch the old oil when it comes out, replace the oil filter, and then you pour in new oil. It's an easy process that just about anyone can follow.

Usually, a mechanic will charge you around $50 dollars for this simple task. That's right, $50 for 15 minutes of their time. They're not charging you for the work they just did — they're charging you for their experience and all the years they spent learning their craft.

If you're amazing at something that you focused on for years, you need to charge what you're worth. Once you raise your prices, customers will notice that you take pride in what you do. They'll make a more serious consideration before buying your product or service because now they're investing a larger portion of their money into you. This helps filter out serious customers from those who just want to waste your time.

You need to charge your price with the utmost confidence. The minute you start to budge and offer a lower price, your customer will start to doubt your work and value.

You need to charge what you're worth and adjust that price depending on the value of the business you're working with. What do I mean by that? Let's assume that you're a freelance graphic designer. You're making a logo for a lawn care business in your town and charging them $3,000 because that's your set price. One day your phone rings and it's a billion-dollar company that wants to work with you. Are you going to charge this company your set price of $3,000? NO! The value of this company is worth BILLIONS, so your price better be somewhere in the millions.

This is why you need to figure out how you're going to charge your prices. Not every business is worth the same. You wouldn't charge a local lawn care business the same that you would charge a billion-dollar company — that would be stupid. A lot of this also depends on the product or service that you're trying to sell.

You wouldn't price a monthly program the same way you would a one-time purchase. There's usually two ways that people charge for their services, and that's either through a flat rate or by the hour. Which way you choose ultimately depends on your business and financial needs. I run a web design business, so I tend to charge a flat rate because it's what works best for me.

Whether you charge a flat rate or by the hour, know your worth. When I first started my business, my prices were way too low because I was afraid that no one would buy my service if I charged a higher price. The moment I noticed what people were willing to pay for my work is when I realized my value and raised my prices accordingly. Everyone in this world has problems, and everyone in this world is willing to pay someone to solve those problems. Offer a solution at the price of your knowledge and experience.

THE POWER OF WORDS.

Earlier we talked about verbal and nonverbal communication, but did you know that the actual words you use also play a huge role in whether you're able to persuade someone or not?

Whenever you're talking to a potential client, you want to make sure that you choose your words carefully. Sometimes we use everyday words and phrases that carry huge meanings. Let's assume that you're having a meeting with a customer and you're trying to persuade them to buy your service. The two of you have been talking for a while now and suddenly, they have a question and you start off your answer with something like this:

"Let me be honest with you..."

Saying this is a bad move. What are you trying to say? That you've been lying to them this entire time?

Using a small phrase like that can cost you an entire sale. It triggers our brain to put up defenses, so we automatically become suspicious. Words are powerful and that's why it's important to know how and when to use them.

If you're writing a book, making an advertisement, or creating a blog post, you need to know who your target audience is. If you know who your target audience is, you're able to construct your words more effectively. This book uses a lot of informal language and it's easy to understand; that's because this book is targeted towards a general audience. If I started throwing out statistics and all these other sophisticated terms, then this book would be targeted more towards scholars. The way you word things is crucial and powerful.

In business, you want to be as clear and concise as possible; this means you shouldn't confuse others.

A lot of times, freelancers will try to explain all the technicalities to you. This is very common in the world of IT. A mom will try to find a web developer to make a small website for her gardening business and next thing you know, some web developer is trying to explain relational database management systems to her. Listen — SHE DOESN'T CARE. She doesn't want to know what any of that is; she just wants a website for her flowers!

If you're working in a certain field, you're working there because you understand it; the customer already knows this. There's no need to try and awe them with your intelligence and sophisticated words — it doesn't work. If anything, it confuses them because customers don't care about any of that; they just want to know if they can trust you to deliver a valuable product or service to them. The words and phrases you use should be effective, persuasive, clear, and simple to digest.

Earlier I gave you an example of a short yet powerful phrase that you should never say to customers. Here are some more examples of words and quotes that you should try to avoid in the world of sales:

"Sorry to bother you."

You'll hear this one a lot in cold calls. First of all, why are you apologizing? You're essentially telling them that you're bothering them. Influence is all about having a higher status than the other person. By apologizing, you're bringing down your power and self-worth. Don't apologize. If you feel like you're wasting their time, then why are you talking to them in the first place?

"Contract."

If you run a freelancing business, you'll probably have some sort of paperwork that your client signs in order to finalize a transaction or agree to a set of terms and conditions.

Usually, this is in the form of a contract. The problem with this word is that it sounds intimidating. What comes to mind when you think of a contract? Probably important papers that a judge would make you sign, right? The word sounds like too huge of a commitment and it's too serious. Instead, you want to use the word "agreement." This sounds a lot less tedious and intimidating.

"Hey, I haven't heard back from you!"

You want to avoid saying this at all costs because you're stating the obvious. This phrase sounds confrontational and needy. Don't try to make your prospect feel guilty. Figure out what you did wrong and focus on that. If you couldn't get that client, don't sweat it. You're not going to close every sale. Learn from your mistakes and keep searching. There are thousands of potential clients out there. Don't force a sale — it just makes you look desperate.

"Buy."

Wait, isn't that what business is all about? Buying? Although this might be true, that word carries a bad reputation. EVERYONE loves to own things, but NOBODY likes to buy things. When we hear that word, we immediately start to think of money. Use a more enticing word like "own" or "take" instead.

You see how powerful words are? Once you understand this, you start paying more attention to what you're saying. Sometimes, it's not your product or service that isn't selling — it's the way you're trying to sell it. Persuasion is about using the right words and knowing when to use them. This is why practicing out loud is crucial; you get to hear everything you're saying. Get rid of unnecessary words and implement powerful and persuasive ones instead. You want to know exactly how to respond to every objection that is thrown at you.

THE FIVE OBSTACLES.

This whole chapter has revolved around sales strategies and ways to get people to buy your product or service, but why exactly DO people buy? There are five main reasons why people DON'T buy things. If people aren't buying your product or service, this is why:

Lack of need!

If you go to a store and find a TV but already have one at home, are you going to buy it? Probably not. Why? You don't need it! Why are you going to buy something that you don't need? Sometimes, it's as simple as that! You can't persuade someone to buy your product or service if they feel like they don't need it. Save your time and leave these types of people alone.

Lack of desire!

The second reason people don't buy things is because they have no desire.

Close your eyes and imagine a plain steak with no seasoning. You have no desire for one, right? Now, close your eyes and imagine a super juicy and tender steak with the perfect amount of seasoning. Unless you're a vegan, you're probably feeling a strong desire for one now. If you present your product or service in a boring way, your prospect has no desire to buy it. Make your product or service compelling and irresistible. You want to give your prospect a strong reason to desire it.

Not a priority!

If something isn't a priority, we tend to just leave it there; we don't act on it because there's a lack of urgency. If you're a student and I give you a paper to write today, you probably won't do it. If I tell you it's due tomorrow morning, you're going to run for a pencil. Until you give your prospect a reason on why they need to buy NOW, they won't act.

There's no money!

This is the most obvious reason why people don't buy things. If you don't buy something, it's probably because you can't afford it. If you're a freelancer, you tend to hear this reason a lot when you try to work with a small business ran by a single person. You want to avoid approaching people who can't afford your product or service. Sometimes, people DO have money, but they'll lie about it. When they say this, it usually means that they don't see any value in your product or service. Make them see the value. If you're selling to another business, make them see it as an investment. You add value to something by adding a story to it. If I try to sell you a regular pen, it serves no purpose other than to write with. What if that pen was the exact same one that a past President used? Now it has a story behind it and carries value. You want to make your work valuable.

Zero trust!

Unless you're talking to a prospect who's familiar with you or has worked with you in the past, they aren't going to trust you in the beginning. You're a complete stranger to them and you're expecting them to just give you money in exchange for a product or service? The whole idea sounds so absurd! If you close a sale, that's because the person trusts you. Sometimes you'll have prospects who'll give you their full trust right off the bat, while other times you'll have to work for it. How do you gain their trust? Social proof! Show them your portfolio and past clients you've worked with. Show them a few of your testimonials. Show them past case studies so they can see what you're capable of. You build trust by being open and honest. A lot of times, people decide whether to trust you or not depending on how they see you. Appearance plays a huge role in how people perceive us.

MIRRORING.

How many times have you been outside and seen somebody like you? Immediately, you sort of like them a little; you share something in common. Think of all your friends right now. How did you first become friends? Probably by sharing things in common, right?

Whenever we see someone who reminds us of ourselves, our brain automatically favors them. If I see someone wearing a shirt with a band I like, I want to talk to that person. This same principle applies to the world of business.

You want to mirror your prospect to gain their trust and create a relationship. This is done by learning about the person you're meeting beforehand. Figure out what they like. What's their personality? The best way you can mirror a prospect is by wearing clothes that match the situation and setting.

As a web designer, what I wear depends on who I'm meeting. If I'm going to meet an attorney, I might wear dress pants and dress shoes. Imagine if I was going to meet with a gym owner and wore that same outfit — I'd look ridiculous! It's too formal. You need to dress accordingly and blend into your environment.

Small talk is just as important. Personally, I'm someone who hates small talk; I want to have meaningful and deep conversations, but if you're meeting with a prospect, you don't want jump right into the sale — it makes you look desperate. You should spend a minute or two talking casually to your prospect to show them that you genuinely care. Pay attention to their behavior and know how to reciprocate. The more you start to pick up on these nuances, the easier it becomes to communicate with various types of personalities. What you wear and how you speak can affect whether you close or not.

Living Actively

Nowadays, everyone is always busy working or running their business. Unless you're an athlete, you're probably not doing much for your overall health.

Getting money caters the mind. If you're not getting enough money, your mind feels stressed; if you're getting a lot of money, your mind feels calm. We get so caught up in catering the mind that we forget to cater the body. You might be financially free, but what good is that if your body isn't healthy? In order to experience TRUE happiness, you need to take care of your body and mind. The heart is like a locked door that needs two keys to open; one key comes from the mind and the other comes from the body. You can't expect to fully open that door with just one key — you need both.

Exercising regularly and eating the right things is crucial in order to keep the body healthy. Your body is a sanctuary that should be treated with respect. If you don't respect it, no one else will. Disease doesn't care that you're making a lot of money or working a successful job; if your body is unhealthy, it's going to take you.

Think of your body like a car. What does a car need? Maintenance. If you regularly maintain and take care of your car, it'll run for a long time. What happens if you stop taking care of your car? It starts to break down. You need to constantly be moving and feeding your body with the nutrients that it needs in order to perform optimally. If you work in a setting where you're always sitting down, you need to exercise. Did you know that an estimated 300,000 deaths happen a year due to obesity? This deadly disease can lead to other complications in the future like heart disease, diabetes, and even cancer.

Despite all of this, why is it that we continue to ignore our bodies? It's all you have; you're slowly killing yourself by trashing your body with sugar, processed foods, and drugs. Get up and move. Sprint, lift weights, ride a bike, play a sport. Whatever you do, you need to stay active. As a web designer who works from home, I'm constantly in front of my screen. I understand the dangers of living a sedentary lifestyle, so I make it a priority to constantly exercise and stick to a good nutrition plan.

How many of your coworkers or friends are obese? Are YOU obese? How do you feel about it? If you're obese and you're not doing anything about it, it's because you're okay with it. You're okay with getting heart disease and dying of a stroke. You're okay with disrespecting your body and killing yourself. There's NOTHING okay or beautiful about being obese. You're being dishonest to yourself and ignoring the facts.

Why are you so obsessed with money if you're slowly killing your body? You'll never get the chance to enjoy your wealth because you'll be dead. Be honest with yourself. If your body isn't how you want it to be, ask yourself why. Look at the facts and admit that it's YOUR fault. YOU decided to sit down all day. YOU decided to shove a lot of food down your throat.

As harsh as all of this sounds, you can't run away from the truth. This book is about wealth, financial freedom, and happiness. How can you be rich and happy if you can't touch your own toes? Leigh Hunt once said:

"The groundwork of all happiness is good health."

If you're healthy and active, you feel amazing. You're able to do things and you're in a better mood. Aside from the obvious health benefits to your body, exercising is a catharsis.

Let's say that you're someone who constantly feels stressed from working. If you let that stress build up, it damages your body AND mind. Exercise is amazing because it helps you release stress and it gives you energy. Your body releases endorphins when you exercise; these chemicals interact with your brain and trigger positive emotions that are very similar to that of morphine. This boosts your overall happiness.

Just like maintaining a business, exercising regularly takes a lot of work, discipline, and self-control; you master these skills through action. If exercising was easy, then everyone you know would be shredded and lean. Like I stated in the beginning of this book: humans love taking the easy route. Exercising and eating both make us happy, but eating is easier, so we take that route instead. It's difficult to get home after a long day of work and then pick up some weights or get on the treadmill.

You need to quit making excuses and do something about it. No matter how tired you feel, push yourself. Break past your plateaus and embrace the struggle. If you're willing to give your business or passion 100%, then you need to give exercising 110%. The discipline and self-control that you gain from exercising translates into the workplace.

The body needs as much attention as the mind does. Make it a lifestyle to constantly exercise. Although it may be difficult at first, nothing is instantaneous. It takes consistency and dedication to break old habits and create new ones. The more you do it, the healthier you become. Exercise is just part of it; you also need to make sure you're eating the things your body needs in order to create energy. Give your body the respect it deserves because it's what keeps you breathing and alive. Your body is all you got.

Giving Back to Others

When you first start making money, it feels good. I remember mowing my neighbor's lawn for the first time when I was 13. At the time, I didn't have a lawn tractor, so I had to use a push mower. Being outside in the blazing heat and doing grueling work all for $25 quickly made me learn the value of a dollar. As a teenager, that money felt like a lot to me, so I was excited every time I had to mow the neighbor's lawn.

You don't strive for a better life until you do labor that makes you appreciate the value of a dollar. Once you realize how grueling the work is, you learn to respect others who do it for a living. It's important not to forget where you or your family started. You need to stay in touch with those roots and aim to help those who are still stuck in those positions.

Usually, we don't do that. We start making good money and begin to lose touch with reality. We forget where we started or disconnect with the people who believed in us. I personally think that EVERYONE who has a sustainable income should donate a portion of their money to a cause of their liking. When you give back to others, you feel good, both emotionally and physically.

Giving back to others doesn't always mean you have to give your money away. There are other ways you can help, such as by giving your time and volunteering. When you give back to others without expecting anything in return, it helps you stay in touch with reality; you remember that there are people out there struggling financially or emotionally. People like this often need support in order to give them hope and motivation to help them get back on their feet. Giving back to others also helps your wealth grow, flourish, and prosper.

There was once a story about a young fool who never had to work because of his family's wealth. The years passed and his parents eventually died, leaving him with a huge inheritance. Because the fool had never worked a day in his life, he didn't know the value of money. The fool quickly became obsessed with money and despite his immense wealth, he never gave any to the poor. There was an old man in town who always begged for money. The fool always shunned this old man and refused to give him anything. Eventually, the fool went broke and was forced to beg on the streets. One day, the fool came across the old man who once begged for money. The old man was wearing a suit and eating an apple. He looked down at the fool who was once rich, smirked, and continued on his walk. The old man lived the rest of his life with wealth and the fool died poor. Greed, in the end, fails even the greedy.

This story teaches us the evils of greed. Just because you have a lot of money right now doesn't mean you can't lose it all. Just because a man on the street has nothing right now doesn't mean he can't become richer than you one day. Nothing is forever; everything is constantly changing. Don't waste the fruits of your hard work; instead, share those fruits with the poor so that seeds of wealth, hope, and wisdom may be planted in their hearts.

Money and power lead to financial wealth, but compassion and selflessness lead to emotional wealth. You need to find the perfect balance between the two and stay there. Donate to a charity, volunteer at a dog shelter, pay for someone's meal. The whole goal is to give back to others and expect nothing in return. Anne Frank said it best:

"No one has ever become poor by giving."

Do Something

This book is a combination of everything needed in order to reach financial and emotional freedom. Bliss is the culmination of having everything in life under control and knowing how to deal with problems when they arise.

You are in control of your life but not of your surroundings. Because of this, you will always encounter conflicts and barriers; the important thing is knowing how to get over those obstacles. If you want to be wealthy, you need to work for it. If you want to be fit, you need to work for it. If you want to pay off your debt, you need to work for it. Nothing in this life comes free; everything is a result of hard work and sacrifices. If you truly want something, then you'll do the best you can in order to attain it.

Action makes the difference between a dream and a reality. This whole book is full of information and motivation that anyone can take in; what you do with it is up to you. Do I see myself as a prophet who has life figured out? No! I'm still learning every single day. This book won't change your life unless you decide to work hard and continue learning. Whenever I want something, I go for it. I'm aware that I'll fail a million times before I get there, but I know that it's possible. You need to have that kind of mindset if you want to achieve anything in your life.

Do whatever makes you happy. Just like everyone else in this world, you are meaningless. It's up to you to discover yourself and figure out what your purpose is. You'll never get to accomplish everything, so do as much as you can with the time you have and give it your all. Always do your best and everything else will fall into place. Freedom is a mindset.